NETWORKING
Fishing for Business

Kyle Terry

Edition
Approved Paperback-Edition June 2023
Copyright © 2023 cub & calf,
Laurenson, Spilstr. 2, 14195 Berlin,
Germany
All rights reserved.
ISBN 9798395555212

Contents

A Primer to Networking 5
What is Networking? 5
Why You Should Network 5
A Short How-to Guide... 6

Ready, Steady, Goals 8

Approaching New Contacts 9
Identify the Key Decision-Makers 9
Create a Personalized Value Proposition 11
Offer Value 14

Networking in Person 16
Attend Events.. 16
Be Approachable... 17
Be Authentic.. 18

Networking Online 19
Utilize Your Platform 19
Promoting a product online 21
Networking on LinkedIn.. 23
Networking on Facebook.. 24
Instagram, Twitter, TikTok, and Co 25
Instagram 25
Twitter 26
TikTok 27

- *Meetup* *27*
- *Slack* *27*
- *Discord* *28*

Follow Up 28
Maintain Connections 29
Tips for Shy People 31
How to Network in Different Industries 33
- Networking as a Student 33
- Networking as a Small Business Owner 34
- Networking as an Entrepreneur 35
- Networking as a Lawyer 36
- Networking as a Scientist 38
- Networking in the Film Industry 40
  - *How to Find an Agent?* *41*
- Networking as an Artist 43
- Networking as a Parent 44

A Primer to Networking

What is Networking?

Networking refers to the practice of building and maintaining professional relationships with other individuals and organizations. It is an essential aspect of personal and professional development that involves cultivating a diverse range of contacts, establishing trust and rapport with them, and leveraging these relationships to achieve various goals.

Networking can help you find new job openings, clients, business partners, and other opportunities that you might not have access to otherwise. By expanding your network, you can tap into a wider pool of resources and knowledge, which can be invaluable in achieving your goals.

Networking also allows you to learn from the experiences and expertise of others. By connecting with professionals in your field, you can gain insights into industry trends, best practices, and emerging technologies that can help you improve your skills and stay competitive.

Building a strong network of contacts can also provide you with emotional and social support. Whether you need advice, feedback, or just a sounding board, having a network of trusted colleagues and mentors can help you navigate challenging situations and overcome obstacles.

Networking can also help you build your reputation and establish yourself as an authority in your field. By connecting with other professionals and demonstrating your expertise, you can gain credibility and recognition within your industry.

Why You Should Network

Networking can benefit anyone, regardless of their career stage, industry, or job title.

Networking should become part of your everyday life.

For example, students can connect with peers, professors, and professionals in their field to gain knowledge about job prospects, industry trends, and career paths.

Job seekers can network with recruiters or hiring managers to find job leads, get referrals, and learn more about potential employers.

Professionals in any field can use their networking skills to expand their knowledge and skills, build relationships with colleagues and mentors, and advance their careers.

Entrepreneurs can network to find potential investors, partners, and customers, as well as to gain insights into the market and industry.

Networking can help freelancers and creatives find new clients, sell their work, build their reputation, and expand their professional network.

Business owners can find potential clients, partners, and investors, as well as gain insights into the market and industry through networking.

In short, anyone who wants to develop their professional network and gain a competitive edge can benefit from networking. It's an essential skill that can help you achieve your goals, grow your career, and create meaningful connections with others.

In the final chapter of this book, I have compiled some networking ideas for specific jobs and industries, but the core ideas can be applied for anyone in any situation.

A Short How-to Guide

Overall, networking is important because it can help you achieve your personal and professional goals, improve your knowledge and skills, and provide you with support and opportunities throughout your career. If done right, it can expand your career prospects, and grow your social circle. Here is a short step-by-set guide on how to approach networking. More in-depth advice follows in the later chapters.

1. Define your goals: Before you start networking, clarify what you want to achieve. Are you looking for a job, seeking advice, or trying to establish connections in your industry? Knowing your objectives will help you focus your efforts and approach networking with purpose.
2. Attend events: Look for industry events, seminars, conferences, and workshops in your area or online. These events provide opportunities to meet like-minded professionals and expand your network. Be sure to bring plenty of business cards and be prepared to engage in conversations with others.
3. Be approachable: Approachability is key to networking success. Smile, make eye contact, and be genuinely interested in others. Ask open-ended questions to encourage conversation and show that you are a good listener. Avoid being overly self-promotional and focus on building strong connections.
4. Be authentic: Authenticity is crucial in networking. Be genuine, transparent, and true to yourself. Avoid being overly aggressive or pushy, as it can backfire. Building authentic connections can lead to long-lasting and meaningful professional relationships.
5. Utilize online platforms: Social media platforms like LinkedIn, Twitter, and Facebook can be powerful tools for networking. Create a professional online presence, connect with others in your field, join industry-specific groups, and participate in discussions. Be sure to maintain a professional and polished profile.
6. Follow up: After meeting someone at an event or connecting online, follow up with them within a reasonable timeframe. Send a personalized email or message to express your appreciation for the conversation and express your interest in staying in touch. Remember to be polite, professional, and respectful of their time.
7. Offer value: Networking is not just about taking; it's also about giving. Offer help, advice, or resources to others without expecting

anything in return. Providing value to your network can help you establish yourself as a trusted and reliable professional.

8. Maintain relationships: Building a network is an ongoing process. Stay in touch with your contacts, congratulate them on their achievements, and offer support when needed. Consider scheduling regular check-ins or attending industry events regularly to nurture your relationships.

Remember that networking takes time and effort, and it's important to be patient and persistent. Building a strong professional network provides you with valuable opportunities, support, and resources throughout your career.

Ready, Steady, Goals

Making money should not be your primary goal when networking. Search deeper.

The goals you set for networking will depend on your individual situation and what you hope to achieve.

If you are just starting out in your career or looking to meet new people, your goal may be to expand your professional network by connecting with people in your industry or field.

Once you have found your path you might be faced with a particular challenge in your career or business. Then your goal may be to network with trusted colleagues or mentors who can provide support and advice.

Are support from colleagues and mentors not enough and you are looking for a new job? Your goal may be to network with recruiters, hiring managers, and other professionals who can help you learn about job openings.

If you want to learn more about your industry, maybe to establish yourself as an authority in your field or find clients to grow your business, your goal may be to network with people who can give insights into trends, best practices, and emerging technologies, build your personal brand, and establish credibility, or find buyers for your product.

Once you know what you want to achieve, it is time to look for the best person to contact and add to your net. This might be either companies, agencies, and other businesses that can help you build your own brand or business, or specific people like clients for your products, teachers, and other experts to learn from, or creatives to build a team for your next project.

Be as precise as possible and note down names and contact details, however, do not just cold call and offer your services or ask for a favor. You need to build a relationship that is based on mutual benefits. Keep on reading for more.

Approaching New Contacts

Identify the Key Decision-Makers

Identifying the key decision-makers within a big client's organization, a future employer, or a distributor of your goods is a critical step in approaching them for networking or business purposes. Approaching a big client can be intimidating, but with careful planning and preparation, you can increase your chances of success.

Before reaching out to a big client, potential employer, or customer, thoroughly research their business, industry, and needs. Understand their pain points, challenges, and goals, and tailor your approach accordingly. This shows that you are genuinely interested and invested in their success.

Look up the company's website, annual reports, or other publicly available information to understand its organizational structure. Identify the key roles and positions that are likely to have decision-making authority related to your product or service.

Whilst many companies, especially big ones, won't publish a list of their employees including individual contact details, platforms like LinkedIn can be a valuable resource for identifying decision-makers within a company. Search for the company on LinkedIn and review the profiles of employees to identify those with relevant job titles, such as executives, managers, or department heads.

Industry events and conferences can be a great occasion to network and connect with decision makers in person. Attend relevant events and make a point to engage in conversations and exchange contact information with executives, managers, or other key personnel from the big client's organization.

If you have existing contacts or customers within the same industry or market, ask for referrals to decision-makers. Referrals can often open doors and provide valuable introductions.

If you are unable to identify key decision-makers through research or networking, consider reaching out to the company directly. Call or email the company's general contact or customer service and inquire about the relevant contact person or department for your product or service.

Many industries have professional directories or databases that list key personnel within companies. These directories can be helpful in identifying decision-makers and their contact information.

Stay updated on the big client's news, press releases, and updates to identify key decision-makers who may be mentioned in these communications. This can help you identify relevant contacts and establish a point of reference in your approach.

Remember that different companies may have different decision-making structures, so it's important to tailor your approach based on the specific organization. Once you have identified key decision-makers, you can tailor your networking or business approach accordingly to increase your chances of success.

Create a Personalized Value Proposition

Crafting a compelling value proposition is essential when approaching a new business partner or potential customer. It's important to clearly communicate the value that you, your product, or service can offer to the client. Focus on the benefits and outcomes your offering can deliver, rather than just listing features.

Research and understand the client's industry, market, challenges, and pain points. What are their specific needs or problems that your product or service can address? The better you understand their needs, the more targeted and effective your value proposition can be.

Look for shared interests, experiences, or connections that you can use to establish a rapport with the client. This could be a mutual contact, a similar industry background, or a common interest. Use this shared ground as an icebreaker to start the conversation.

What sets your product or service apart from the competition? Identify the unique features, benefits, or advantages that your offering provides, like cost savings, increased efficiency, improved performance, enhanced customer experience, or any other value proposition that is relevant to the client.

Highlight the positive outcomes or results that the new client can achieve by using your product or service, for example increased revenue, reduced costs, improved productivity, expanded market share, or any other tangible benefits that are meaningful to the client.

Keep your value proposition simple, clear, and easy to understand. Avoid jargon or technical language that may confuse the client. Use language that resonates with the client's industry or market and focus on the value that your product or service can bring.

Frame your value proposition from the perspective of the big client. Show how your product or service can specifically address their needs and provide value to their business. Use language that demonstrates that you understand their challenges and can supply a solution that meets their requirements.

Show confidence in yourself and your offering and convey enthusiasm for working with the big client. Positive energy and genuine excitement can be contagious and help you build rapport.

Share testimonials, case studies, or success stories from previous clients or customers to provide social proof of your capabilities and build credibility.

Here are some examples for value propositions that you can adjust to your needs:

> "Our new hoover is designed to make cleaning your home effortless and efficient. With powerful suction technology, it easily picks up dirt, dust, and debris from carpets, hardwood floors, and even hard-to-reach places. Its lightweight design and flexible hose make it easy to maneuver and clean under furniture and tight spaces, while its washable filter ensures optimal performance every time. Say goodbye to bulky, heavy vacuums and hello to a cleaner, healthier home with our new hoover."

"My new novel is an immersive and captivating story that will transport you/the reader to another world. With vivid descriptions and relatable characters, it will keep you turning the pages until the very end. Set in a distant, fantastical land, the story weaves together adventure, romance, and mystery in a way that will leave you wanting more. Whether you're looking for an escape from reality or a thought-provoking journey, my new novel has something for everyone. Join me on a thrilling ride that will leave you breathless and wanting more."

"I am a biological science graduate with a strong academic background in biology and hands-on experience in laboratory research. With a proven ability to design and execute experiments, analyze data, and communicate results, I will bring a wealth of expertise and knowledge to your scientific team. My attention to detail, critical thinking skills, and collaborative mindset make me an asset to any research project, and my dedication to advancing the field of biology is second to none. Whether you're looking to add a talented researcher to your team or partner with a passionate and skilled scientist on your next project, I am the perfect candidate for you."

Consider the most appropriate communication channel to reach out to the contact, such as email, LinkedIn, other networking platforms, or in person. Choose a channel that aligns with their preferences and the nature of your relationship.

Avoid generic or template messages when reaching out (make sure to adjust the above examples and be specific about your talents or product). Craft a personalized message, use their name, mention specific details, and show that you have tailored your approach to them.

In your message, introduce yourself and briefly explain your professional background and interests. Establish common ground, such as shared professional interests, mutual connections, or common experiences, to create a connection and show that you have done your homework. Get it right, as mistakes can get your message quickly transferred to the trash folder.

Clearly state your purpose for reaching out and make a specific request, such as asking for a brief phone call, a coffee chat, or an informational interview. Be respectful of their time and offer flexibility in scheduling.

Continuously test and refine your value proposition based on feedback from potential clients, customers, or other stakeholders. Iterate and improve your value proposition to ensure it resonates with your target audience.

Finally, if the contact declines your request or expresses disinterest, respect their decision, and do not push further. Professional networking is voluntary, and not everyone may be interested or available to connect.

Offer Value

Providing value to your network is a key element of effective networking. By offering help, advice, or resources to others without expecting anything in return, you can build trust, establish yourself as a reliable professional, and strengthen your relationships. Here are some tips for offering value in your networking efforts:

Pay attention to the needs and challenges of others in your network. Listen actively during conversations and ask questions to better understand their situation. This will help you identify ways in which you can provide value.

If you have specific expertise or knowledge in a certain area, offer to share it with others in your network. This could be through informal advice, insights, or recommendations that can help others solve problems or achieve their goals.

Be willing to offer your help and support like helping with a project, providing feedback, or volunteering your time or resources. Be genuine in your offer and follow through on your commitments.

Share relevant articles, reports, or other information that may be helpful to others in your network, like news about industry trends, best practices, or new opportunities. Sharing valuable resources demonstrates your willingness to contribute and adds value to your relationships.

If you know of someone who could benefit from connecting with someone else in your network, make introductions through email, social media, or in person. Facilitating introductions can be a powerful way to create mutual value and strengthen relationships.

Be proactive in identifying ways to provide value and authenticity in your intentions. Avoid self-promotion or expecting immediate returns. Instead, focus on genuinely helping others without any expectation of reciprocity.

While offering value, be mindful of others' time and boundaries. Respect their preferences, privacy, and workload. Do not overwhelm them with excessive messages or requests.

Providing value to your network is a win-win approach. It helps you build trust, establish yourself as a helpful and reliable professional, and foster mutually beneficial relationships with others. Remember that effective networking is about building meaningful connections and offering value to others, not just taking from the network.

Networking in Person

Attend Events

Attending industry events, seminars, conferences, and workshops can be an effective way to network. Before attending an event, do your research. Find out the schedule, speakers, and topics to be discussed. This will help you come prepared with relevant questions and talking points.

Business cards are a handy way to exchange contact information with others. Make sure you have enough cards to hand out and keep them easily accessible.

Be ready to introduce yourself concisely and clearly. Develop a brief elevator pitch that highlights your background, skills, and what you're looking for in your networking efforts.

After the event, follow up with the contacts you made. You were hopefully able to collect business cards or contact details yourself, so send personalized emails or connect with them on professional networking platforms, such as LinkedIn. Refer to specific points from your conversation to help them remember you.

It can be helpful to jot down notes about the people you meet and the conversations you have but do this afterwards or in a quiet moment and don't make your new contact feel quizzed and dissected. Taking notes can serve as a reference for future interactions and help you remember important details.

You will find that exposing yourself to more and more interactions will make it easier to relax and be authentic, so don't worry if your nerves show at the beginning or you can't establish a meaningful connection. Just keep on trying, networking is a learning curve just like anything else.

Remember that networking is about building relationships, not just collecting business cards. Focus on building genuine connections, being respectful of others' time, and offering value. Building a strong network takes time and effort, but it can be an asset in your professional career.

Be Approachable

Smile, keep eye contact, ask open-ended questions.

Approachability plays a crucial role in networking success. A warm and friendly smile can create a positive impression and make others feel more comfortable approaching you, which is especially helpful, if you are too shy to make the first step.

Maintaining eye contact during conversations shows that you are attentive and genuinely interested in the person you are speaking with. It conveys respect and builds trust.

Pay attention to what others are saying without distractions. Avoid checking your phone or looking around while someone is speaking to you. Show that you value their input and opinions by giving them your full attention.

Ask open-ended questions that encourage conversation and allow the other person to share about themselves. Listen actively to their responses and show genuine curiosity. Avoid interrupting or constantly talking about yourself.

Be open, approachable, and friendly in your interactions with others. Be willing to initiate conversations and engage with new people. Approach networking with a mindset of building relationships rather than just trying to "get" something from others.

Treat others with respect, regardless of their position, background, or industry. Show kindness, empathy, and professionalism in your interactions. Avoid being overly aggressive, pushy, or disrespectful. Respect differences in opinions, backgrounds, and perspectives, and be willing to engage in deep discussions without being confrontational.

Remember, building meaningful connections is the foundation of networking. By being approachable, genuinely interested in others, and authentic in your interactions, you can establish strong professional relationships that can benefit you in your career and beyond.

Be Authentic

Authenticity is key in networking and should work with approachability hand in hand. Building genuine connections with others is more likely to result in meaningful and long-lasting professional relationships.

> Don't fake it till you make it, but practice.

Be genuine and true to yourself. Avoid trying to be someone you're not or using fake personas to impress others. *Fake it until you make it* is only a poor substitute for genuine interactions. Often "faking it" creates a strange vibe that might not be immediately uncovered but leads to barriers that are difficult to break down later. Authenticity shines through and helps you build trust with others.

Share your own experiences, stories, and perspectives with others. This helps you establish a personal connection and fosters genuine conversations. Don't be afraid to show vulnerability and share your challenges and successes.

Be open and transparent about your goals and expectations when networking. Avoid being overly opportunistic or hiding your true intentions. Building relationships based on transparency and mutual understanding creates a solid foundation for long-term connections.

Authentic networking involves actively listening to others. Show genuine interest in what others have to say and avoid interrupting or monopolizing conversations. Listening attentively helps you understand others better and fosters deeper connections. Ask thoughtful questions, listen actively, and show empathy towards others.

Authenticity builds trust, and trust is crucial in any relationship, including professional ones. Be reliable, keep your promises, and demonstrate integrity in your actions. Building trust takes time, but it's a valuable investment in your networking efforts.

Be consistent in your interactions with others. Avoid being sporadic or only reaching out when you need something. Building authentic connections requires consistent effort and genuine interest in others.

By being authentic in your networking efforts, you can build significant and long-lasting professional relationships that can benefit you and your contacts in the long run. Authenticity creates a solid foundation for trust, mutual respect, and collaboration, which are essential elements of a successful network.

Networking Online

Utilize Your Platform

Online platforms can be powerful tools for networking, especially in today's digital age.

To get yourself ready to network and provide potential connections an overview of your skills you should set up a polished and professional profile on social media platforms like LinkedIn, Twitter, and Facebook. If you are more about visual content and have products to sell or showcase, Instagram or TikTok should be on your list.

Tailor your online presence and messaging to your target audience. Customize your profiles, content, and messages to align with the needs and interests of your target audience, whether it's potential employers, clients, or collaborators.

Use a clear profile picture, include relevant information about your professional background, and highlight your skills and achievements. Identify your unique strengths, skills, and experiences that set you apart from others. Create a personal brand statement that communicates your value proposition and use it consistently across your online presence.

Optimize your profiles with relevant keywords, a professional profile picture, and a compelling summary that highlights your skills, achievements, and aspirations.

Highlight your achievements, projects, and work samples online to demonstrate your skills and expertise. Share your success stories, awards, and testimonials from clients or colleagues to establish your credibility.

Request recommendations and endorsements from colleagues, supervisors, or clients to showcase your skills and credibility. Display them prominently on your online profiles to enhance your reputation.

Just like with any contact, be thoughtful in your connection requests, personalize them, and explain why you are interested in connecting with them.

And most importantly, provide a way that others can contact you. There is no easier way than making yourself available to others when networking.

Join relevant industry-specific groups which can be a great way to connect with like-minded professionals, participate in discussions, and stay updated on industry trends and news. Engage in discussions and share your insights and expertise to establish yourself as a knowledgeable professional. Share valuable and relevant content, such as articles, blog posts, or industry news, on your online profiles.

Remember that your online presence represents your professional brand. Be mindful of the content you post, comments you make, and the image you portray online. Keep it professional and avoid engaging in negative or controversial discussions (unless this is your goal).

Respond to comments, messages, and requests from your connections in a timely and professional manner. Invest time in nurturing and maintaining meaningful connections by staying in touch, offering help, and being supportive.

If you have a product to sell, you can use your networking platforms to showcase anything you've got to potential customers.

Promoting a product online requires a visually appealing and user-friendly website or landing page than just your skills and personal achievements. Similar to your own profile, a product page should clearly communicate the features, benefits, and value proposition and include clear call-to-actions (CTAs) for users to take action. Such CTAs could be a call to "Buy Now" connected to a working link, or to get in touch with further questions.

Optimize your website or landing page for search engines to improve its visibility in search results. Identify relevant keywords and incorporate them in your website's content, meta tags, and URLs. This can help attract organic traffic to your product's online presence.

Social media platforms such as Facebook, Instagram, Twitter, LinkedIn, and YouTube can be powerful channels for promoting your product. Create engaging and shareable content, run targeted ads, and actively engage with your audience to build a community around your product.

Build an email list of interested prospects and customers and use email marketing to regularly communicate with them. Send out newsletters, product updates, and special offers to keep your audience engaged and informed.

Create high-quality and valuable content related to your product, such as blog posts, articles, videos, infographics, and guides. Share this content on your website, social media, and other relevant platforms to attract and engage your target audience.

Identify influencers in your niche who have a large and engaged following and collaborate with them to promote your product. This can help you reach a wider audience and leverage their credibility and influence to generate interest, especially when your own online presence is in its infancy, or online marketing is not your strength.

Invest in online advertising, such as Google Ads, social media ads, or display ads, to increase your product's visibility and reach. Target your ads to your specific audience based on demographics, interests, and behaviors to maximize their effectiveness.

Offer exclusive promotions, discounts, or limited-time offers to incentivize customers to purchase your product online. This can create a sense of urgency and encourage potential customers to take action.

Excellent customer service can generate positive reviews, testimonials, and word-of-mouth marketing for your product. Respond promptly to customer inquiries, address any issues or complaints, and provide exceptional service to build customer loyalty and advocacy.

Regularly monitor and analyze the results of your online promotion efforts using analytics tools. This can help you understand what strategies are working and what can be improved and make data-driven decisions to optimize your promotional and networking activities.

Networking on LinkedIn

LinkedIn is a professional social network with over 774 million members in more than 200 countries and territories. It was designed for networking and career development, with features such as a job board, company pages, and groups focused on specific industries or interests.

You can use it to connect with other professionals, showcase your skills and experience, and find job opportunities or potential clients.

Your LinkedIn profile is your online professional identity. Make sure it is complete, up-to-date, and reflects your skills, experience, and interests. Use a professional profile picture and craft a compelling headline that communicates your value proposition.

Search for professionals in your industry or field and send them personalized connection requests with a brief introduction or a common point of interest. Be respectful of others' privacy settings and only send connection requests to those who are likely to be interested in connecting with you.

Join and actively participate in industry-specific groups on LinkedIn. Share valuable content on your LinkedIn feed, such as articles, blog posts, industry news, and insights, ask questions, and engage in discussions. Engage with others' content by liking, commenting, and sharing. This helps you build relationships, and it also increases your visibility on the platform.

LinkedIn has powerful search filters that allow you to narrow down your search for professionals based on various criteria, such as industry, location, job title, and more. Utilize these filters to find relevant professionals to connect with and expand your network.

Request recommendations from colleagues, clients, or other experts who can speak to your skills and expertise. Additionally, provide recommendations to others whose work you admire to build credibility and establish a positive reputation on LinkedIn.

Networking on Facebook

While Facebook is primarily a social media platform for personal connections, it can also be utilized for professional networking. If you don't want to use your personal profile, you can create a secondary Facebook page that you can access through your private account.

1. Tap in the top right of Facebook.
2. Tap your name at the top.
3. Tap Switch profiles in the top right.
4. Tap Create new profile.
5. Tap Get started, then follow the instructions on the screen to create a profile.

Make sure your Facebook profile is updated and reflects your professional interests, skills, and experiences. Use a professional profile picture and review your privacy settings to ensure that your professional information is visible to the right audience.

Search for and join professional groups on Facebook that are related to your industry or field of interest. These groups can be a valuable source for networking, as you can connect with like-minded people, participate in discussions, and share insights.

Share valuable and relevant professional content on your Facebook timeline, such as industry news, articles, or insights. This can help you showcase your expertise and interests and attract the attention of other professionals. Facebook also allows you to create short videos that will be visible to others via the watch-tab. Include relevant hash keys to increase your visibility and link your Facebook account to your Instagram account, if you have one, to make sharing information between platforms easier.

Like, comment, and share the content of others in your network. Engage in meaningful conversations and provide value through your comments. This can help you build relationships and expand your professional network.

You can send private messages through Facebook Messenger to introduce yourself, ask questions, or request a virtual coffee chat. Be respectful of others' privacy and preferences and personalize your messages for better engagement.

Many professional organizations and groups now host virtual events on Facebook, such as webinars, workshops, and conferences. Attend these events, participate in discussions, and connect with other attendees. Virtual events can be a great way to network and build relationships with others.

While Facebook is a more informal platform, it's important to maintain a professional and authentic tone in your interactions. Avoid controversial or inappropriate content and present yourself in a professional manner.

Instagram, Twitter, TikTok, and Co

Each platform has its own strengths and weaknesses, so it's important to consider your goals, target audience, and content strategy when choosing which platform to use for networking. By leveraging the unique features and strengths of each platform, you can expand your network and reach your goals more effectively.

Instagram can be a powerful tool for networking if used strategically, especially if you lean towards visual content such as photos and videos.

Instagram has a large user base with over 1 billion monthly active users and features such as hashtags, location tags, and tagging other users to increase visibility.

As with all online profiles, make sure your profile is complete and professional-looking. Use a profile picture that represents you or your brand and include a clear bio that describes your expertise, interests, or what you offer.

Hashtags are a great way to reach a wider audience and connect with others who share similar interests. Use relevant hashtags in your posts to increase visibility and attract followers. Instagram allows up to 30 hashtags and you should utilize them all.

Engage with other users by commenting on their posts, responding to their stories, or liking their content. Instagram also offers live sessions of people you want to connect with, leave comments, and share your thoughts to interact with the host and the other viewers.

Collaborate with other Instagram users by participating in giveaways, joint live sessions, or creating content together. This can help you build relationships and increase your visibility.

Twitter can be a great platform for networking if used effectively. Twitter focuses on short-form text-based content called tweets and has a user base of over 330 million monthly active users.

Write short notes about your professional day, include things you have learned, and ask questions. Engage with other users by replying to their tweets, retweeting their content, or liking their posts.

Use relevant hashtags in your tweets to increase visibility and attract followers but try to limit yourself to around 3 hashtags. Make sure that your content is still reader-friendly but do consider attaching a capturing image or GIF to attract the eye.

Twitter chats are live conversations around a specific topic or theme. Participate in relevant Twitter chats to connect with others in your industry or community. Attend Twitter events, such as virtual conferences or tweetups, to meet other Twitter users in person and build relationships.

Create Twitter lists of people or organizations you want to connect with. This can help you stay organized and easily follow their tweets.

TikTok can be a great platform for networking, especially if you're targeting a younger audience or looking to reach people who are interested in visual and creative content. It has a large and growing user base with over 1 billion monthly active users and focuses on short-form video content with a maximum length of 60 seconds.

Use relevant hashtags in your videos to increase visibility and attract followers. TikTok allows up to 100 characters in a hashtag, so you can be quite descriptive with them.

Collaborate with other TikTok users by participating in duets, creating content together, or joining in on challenges such as virtual concerts to meet other users and build relationships.

There are many other online platforms that can be great for networking. Here are a few examples:

Meetup is a platform that helps people find local groups and events based on shared interests or activities. It has over 49 million members in over 190 countries and territories, with groups focused on a wide range of topics, from business and technology to hobbies and social activities.

Slack is a messaging platform designed for teams and communities to communicate and collaborate on projects or interests. It has over 12 million daily active users, with thousands of communities focused on specific industries, interests, or regions.

Discord is a platform that allows users to create or join communities focused on gaming, education, or other interests. It has over 150 million monthly active users, with communities that range from small groups to large communities with thousands of members.

Again, the best platform for networking depends on your goals, industry, and target audience. It's worth exploring different platforms to see which ones resonate with you and offer the best opportunities to expand your network.

> Don't approach anyone through their private accounts. Respect if someone rejects to be contacted via direct messages and seek out other ways of communication.

Follow Up

Following up is a crucial step in networking to maintain and strengthen the connections you've made. After meeting someone at an event or connecting with them online, send a personalized email or message to express your appreciation for the conversation and thank them for their time. Mention something specific that you discussed to show that you were attentive during your interaction.

Follow up within a reasonable timeframe, preferably within 24-48 hours after the initial meeting or connection. This shows that you are proactive and interested in maintaining the connection.

Express your interest in staying in touch and continuing the conversation. Let them know that you value their insights and would like to stay connected for potential future collaborations or opportunities.

Keep your follow-up message polite, professional, and respectful of their time. Avoid using overly casual language or being too pushy. Be mindful of their preferences and communication style.

Offer value in your follow-up message by sharing relevant resources, insights, or information that may be beneficial to the person you are connecting with. This demonstrates your willingness to contribute and provide value in the relationship.

Use the follow-up message as a chance to continue the conversation or suggest a follow-up meeting or call. Be proactive in keeping the communication going and maintaining the momentum of the initial connection.

Avoid using generic or templated messages for follow-ups. Personalize each follow-up message to reflect the specific conversation or interaction you had with the person. This shows that you took the time to remember and acknowledge the details of your conversation.

Following up is essential in networking as it helps in building and maintaining relationships over time. By sending personalized and timely follow-up messages, you can demonstrate your professionalism, sincerity, and interest in fostering meaningful connections with others.

Maintain Connections

Maintaining relationships goes beyond a follow-up and is a crucial aspect of effective networking. Building a network is not a one-

Happy New Year!

time action, but an ongoing process that requires consistent effort and nurturing.

Keep in regular exchange with your contacts, even if it's just a quick email, message, or phone call to say hello or catch up. Times like New Year or other big holiday events are always a good reason to send a short message to stay in touch. Share updates about your professional life and ask about theirs. Show genuine interest in their achievements, challenges, and goals.

When your contacts achieve milestones or successes, congratulate them, and offer your support. Celebrate their accomplishments and show genuine enthusiasm for their achievements. Likewise, when your contacts face challenges or setbacks, offer words of encouragement, empathy, and support.

When your contacts reach out to you for help, be responsive and reliable. Respond to messages and requests in a timely manner and follow through on any commitments you make. Being reliable and dependable builds trust and strengthens your relationships.

Consider scheduling regular check-ins to stay connected. This could be a monthly or quarterly catch-up call, a coffee meeting, or attending industry events together. Regular check-ins help you stay on top of each other's professional updates and maintain a strong connection.

Networking is a two-way street. Look for opportunities to support and help, and also be willing to receive support and assistance when needed. Engage in mutual give-and-take and maintain a balanced and reciprocal relationship.

Remember, maintaining relationships requires consistent effort and genuine interest in others. It's not just about reaching out when you need something, but about nurturing your relationships, and foster a strong and supportive network that can be beneficial in the long run.

Tips for Shy People

If you are an introvert, you might still successfully navigate in person events or take the initiative contacting people online. Take time to recover and recharge after such events and make sure that they are worth your time.

As a shy person you might not even press the send-button for an email. Networking can be challenging for shy people, but it is still possible to build meaningful professional relationships even if you identify as shy.

Begin with small networking events or one-on-one interactions rather than large gatherings or events with big crowds. This can help you feel more comfortable and less overwhelmed.

Set achievable networking goals for yourself, such as initiating conversations with a certain number of people or exchanging contact information with a few new contacts. Celebrate your accomplishments, even if they may seem small.

Prepare in advance by researching the event or the individuals you want to connect with. Having some talking points or questions in mind can help you feel more confident in starting conversations.

Being a good listener is an important networking skill. Focus on the other person, ask open-ended questions, and show genuine interest in their experiences and perspectives.

Take advantage of online networking platforms, where you can connect with professionals and initiate conversations from the comfort of your own space. Online networking can be less intimidating for shy individuals and can provide openings to build relationships at your own pace.

Look for common interests, hobbies, or topics of mutual curiosity to discuss with others. This can help you find common ground and make conversations more enjoyable and engaging.

Consider attending networking events with a friend or colleague who can give support and help you feel more comfortable. Having a familiar face by your side can reduce anxiety and boost your confidence.

Taking care of yourself is important in managing any social anxiety. Make sure to get enough rest, practice relaxation techniques, and engage in activities that help you feel calm and confident before attending networking events.

After networking events or online interactions, follow up with your contacts via email or social media. Sending a personalized message to express your gratitude and interest in maintaining the connection can help solidify the relationship.

Don't try to be someone you're not. Be authentic and true to yourself and focus on building genuine connections rather than trying to impress others. People appreciate authenticity and sincerity.

Remember, networking is about building relationships, and it's okay to take your time and approach it in a way that feels comfortable for you. Don't be too hard on yourself and celebrate your successes, no matter how small they may seem. With practice and persistence, networking can become easier and more enjoyable, even for shy people.

How to Network in Different Industries

Networking as a Student

Networking as a student is important for several reasons. Networking can help you to learn about potential job or internship prospects, and even before you graduate you can build connections with professionals in your field who can help you gain insight into the job market and connect with potential employers.

It is never too late nor too early to start networking.

As a more immediate goal, networking creates opportunities to learn from others, whether it's through attending workshops, participating in online forums, or connecting with other students. Building relationships with experienced professionals can help you gain guidance and mentorship to complete your education with a strong focus on your interests and future possibilities.

But networking is not just useful for professional connections. Networking can provide students with a social support system and connect you with other students or professionals who have similar interests or experiences.

Starting your networking journey early will also help you develop your communication and interpersonal skills so that you become a more confident and effective communicator.

Overall, networking as a student can be a valuable tool for career development, mentorship, learning occasions, social support, and personal development. Besides your chosen lectures, career fairs and job expos are great to connect with potential employers and learn about job and internship prospects outside of your direct university environment. Attending conferences, workshops, or other professional development are already possible as a student and you should ask your professor about them.

Participate in internships or co-op programs to gain experience and build connections with professionals in your field.

You should also look out for professional associations or clubs related to your field of study to meet other students and professionals with similar interests and goals.

Even before you become and alumnus yourself, you can connect with alumni from your school or program for advice about your chosen career path from those who have already graduated. Reach out to them and ask for informational interviews to gain insight into their career paths and learn about potential opportunities.

Networking as a Small Business Owner

As a small business owner, it's important to have a support network of other entrepreneurs, mentors, and advisors to help you grow and expand your business.

Small business associations, such as your local Chamber of Commerce, can offer opportunities to network with other entrepreneurs and find mentors and advisors who can offer guidance and support. These organizations often host events and meetings where you can connect with other business owners and potential clients.

Attend industry events and conferences to meet other business owners and industry experts who can offer advice and support. Be sure to bring plenty of business cards and be prepared to introduce yourself and your business.

Look for online communities and groups for small business owners. These communities can provide a forum for discussion, networking, and learning from others who have experience in your industry.

Look for advisors and mentors who can offer guidance and support as you grow your business. Consider reaching out to industry experts, business coaches, or experienced entrepreneurs who can give valuable insights and advice. Attend workshops and training sessions to learn new skills and techniques that can help you grow your business.

If you are after expanding your client list, identify your ideal client, before networking. Consider factors such as demographics, location, and industry to help you target your networking efforts. Just like collaborators and other professionals, you can meet clients in person at industry events or find groups online.

Remember, building a support network takes time and effort, but it can be incredibly valuable for your business. Be open to learning and seeking advice and be willing to offer help and support in return.

Networking as an Entrepreneur

Networking is a crucial part of building a successful career as an entrepreneur. As an entrepreneur, there are many different types of events you can attend to network and make new connections.

Choose events that are relevant to your industry and business goals, and to be strategic about the events you attend. Look for events that align with your interests, goals, and target audience, and make sure you're prepared to make the most of your time at each event.

Attending industry conferences and trade shows provides breaks to meet other entrepreneurs and professionals in your industry. These events often have keynote speakers, workshops, and panel discussions that can help you stay up-to-date on the latest trends and developments in your field. Many local business organizations and chambers of commerce hold regular networking events such as breakfast meetings or after-work mixers.

Meetups and industry groups are organized around specific topics or industries. Look for local groups on sites like Meetup.com or LinkedIn.

Social events such as fundraisers, galas, and charity events generate chances to meet other professionals in a more relaxed setting.

Pitch competitions and startup events are designed to connect entrepreneurs with investors, mentors, and other entrepreneurs.

After meeting someone at a networking event, follow up with them via email or phone to continue the conversation and explore potential opportunities to work together.

Remember that any event can be a networking occasion if you approach it with the right mindset. Be open to meeting new people, be prepared to talk about your business, and have business cards or other materials ready to share with those you meet.

Networking as a Lawyer

Networking is a critical component of building a successful legal career.

Joining a legal organization can provide valuable networking opportunities. Consider joining a bar association or professional organization in your area or in your practice area. For example, the Intellectual Property Owners Association (IPO) is an organization for IP lawyers. Attend meetings, participate in committees, and engage with other members to build relationships.

There are many legal networking events, such as conferences, seminars, and luncheons, that can give breaks to meet other lawyers and legal professionals. These events often have keynote speakers, workshops, and panel discussions that can help you stay up-to-date on the latest legal developments and trends, as well as meet potential clients.

LinkedIn is a popular online network to connect with other legal professionals. There are also legal forums such as LawLink and Avvo that allow lawyers to ask questions and share their expertise with other lawyers.

Pro Bono organizations are offered through local bar associations, such as the Legal Aid Society, and provide chances for lawyers to volunteer their time to help those who cannot afford legal services. Volunteering can help you build relationships with other lawyers and legal professionals while making a positive impact in your community.

Bar associations are professional organizations for lawyers that offer continuing legal education courses, and other resources for lawyers. Examples include the American Bar Association (ABA) and state or local bar associations.

When considering which legal organizations or online networks to join, think about your specific goals and interests as a lawyer. Consider what practice areas you're interested in, what type of clients you want to work with, and what networking events or online networks will help you achieve those goals.

The American Bar Association (ABA) is one of the largest and most well-known legal organizations in the United States. It offers a variety of networking opportunities, including conferences, seminars, and online communities for lawyers in different practice areas.

The National Association of Criminal Defense Lawyers (NACDL) is an organization for criminal defense lawyers that provides networking occasions, training programs, and resources to help lawyers stay up-to-date on the latest developments in criminal law.

The Women in Law Empowerment Forum (WILEF) is an organization that supports the advancement of women in the legal profession. It provides networking chances, mentorship programs, and other resources to help women lawyers achieve their professional goals.

Remember that networking as a lawyer is about building long-term relationships and establishing yourself as a trusted and knowledgeable resource for your clients and colleagues. Be genuine, be professional, and be strategic about your networking efforts to make the most of your time and build strong relationships with other legal professionals.

Networking as a Scientist

The scientific field is very competitive, especially if you want to establish yourself as a leading scientist with your own projects.

As you walk through your early science career, attending conferences and events should be part of your yearly routine. These events provide opportunities to meet other scientists in your field, learn about the latest research, and build relationships with potential collaborators.

Collaborating with other scientists is an effective way to build your network. Reach out to colleagues who share your research interests and explore potential collaborations, either in person, during conferences, or via email and other networks such as ResearchGate.

Look for other scientists who are working on similar research questions or who have complementary expertise. Once you've identified potential collaborators, reach out to them to introduce yourself and discuss potential collaboration prospects. Start by sending an email or scheduling a call to discuss your research interests and potential areas of collaboration.

Once you've established a connection with potential collaborators, work together to develop a shared research question or project. Be open to different perspectives and ideas and be willing to compromise to find common ground.

Clearly define the roles and responsibilities of each collaborator to ensure that everyone is working towards the same goals. Be transparent about expectations and deadlines and establish a communication plan to ensure that everyone is kept up-to-date on the project's progress.

Collaborative research projects often require funding, so be sure to identify potential funding sources and work together to develop a grant proposal.

Regular communication is essential to the success of a research collaboration. Schedule regular check-ins and progress updates and be open and honest with your collaborators about any challenges or obstacles that arise. Successful collaborations require mutual respect, open communication, and a willingness to work towards common goals.

Joining a scientific society or association can provide valuable networking opportunities. These organizations often host events, workshops, and meetings that bring together scientists from different institutions and disciplines. Many scientific communities are now also online, such as ResearchGate or LinkedIn groups for scientists, and provide a platform to connect with other researchers, share your work, and ask questions.

Volunteering for scientific organizations is a great chance to meet other scientists and contribute to the scientific community. Consider volunteering for a scientific society, serving on a committee, or organizing an event.

Networking with scientists outside your field creates new perspectives and insights that can benefit your research. Attend interdisciplinary events or join interdisciplinary research groups.

Remember, when networking as a scientist, it's important to be genuine, respectful, and professional. Listen to others, share your expertise, and be open to new ideas and collaborations. With these tips, you can build a strong network of colleagues and collaborators in your field.

Networking in the Film Industry

Breaking into the film industry can be challenging, but with determination, perseverance, and the right strategies, it is possible to pursue a successful career in this competitive field.

Once you are sure to have acquired the necessary skills and knowledge for the specific field you want to enter, create a portfolio that showcases your work and skills. This could include a demo reel, a resume, a website, or samples of your work. Your portfolio should demonstrate your talent, creativity, and professionalism, and should be tailored to the specific field or job you are interested in.

On your journey to acquire the skills and credentials, keep in mind to already create a network of other likeminded professionals. Just like a student, reach out to people who have trodden the same path before you, attend industry events, film festivals, workshops, and other relevant gatherings to meet and connect with professionals in the field.

Build relationships with industry insiders, make connections, and seek advice or mentorship from experienced individuals. Utilize online platforms like LinkedIn, social media, and professional organizations to expand your network.

Seek opportunities to gain practical experience in the film industry. This could include internships, volunteer work, or low-budget projects. Look for openings to work on set, assist with productions, or collaborate with other filmmakers to gain hands-on experience and build your resume. Sometimes, working your way in from other branches that are easier to access is a good strategy, such as signing up with agencies as a background actor.

Take the initiative and create your own projects to showcase your skills and creativity. This could be short films, web series, or other independent productions. Creating your own projects not only helps you gain practical experience but also demonstrates your initiative and dedication to the industry.

The film industry is constantly evolving, and it's important to stay up-to-date with the latest trends, technologies, and industry news. Follow industry publications, websites, blogs, and social media accounts such as IMDB, Backstage, or the Hollywood Reporter, to stay informed about the latest developments in the film industry.

Breaking into the film industry can be tough, and rejection is common. Be prepared for setbacks and challenges and develop a resilient mindset to persevere through them. Keep honing your skills, networking, and seeking opportunities, and don't give up on your passion and goals.

Breaking into the film industry requires determination, hard work, and perseverance. By gaining relevant skills, building a portfolio, networking, gaining practical experience, creating your own projects, staying informed, and maintaining persistence, you can increase your chances of success in this competitive field.

How to Find an Agent? Finding a talent agent or representation can be an important step in advancing your career in the film, television, or entertainment industry. This also includes creatives of the written word who want to traditionally publish books with major publishers.

Research talent agencies that specialize in your field or niche within the entertainment industry. Look for reputable and established agencies that have a track record of representing talent similar to your skills and experience. Make sure the agency is legitimate and has a good reputation in the industry.

Attend industry events, such as film festivals, workshops, seminars, and networking events, where you may have the chance to meet agents or talent managers in person. Make sure to come prepared with your portfolio, resume, and elevator pitch to showcase your skills and leave a positive impression.

Many talent agencies have online platforms where you can submit your materials for consideration. Research and identify agencies that accept online submissions and follow their submission guidelines carefully. You may need to submit your resume, headshot, demo reel, or other materials as per their requirements.

Networking is key in the entertainment industry. Connect with industry professionals from different fields, such as actors, directors, producers, or casting directors, who may have connections to talent agents.

Ask for recommendations from other talent professionals or colleagues who already have representation. They may be able to recommend a reputable agent or talent manager who they have worked with or know personally. Personal recommendations can carry weight and help you get your foot in the door.

Some talent agencies accept unsolicited submissions, where you can send your materials directly to them without a referral. Follow their submission guidelines carefully, be professional and concise in your submission, highlighting your skills, experience, and what makes you unique.

Finding the right agent may take time and effort, so be prepared to be patient and persistent. Follow up on your submissions but do so in a professional and respectful manner. Many agencies recommend waiting at least 3-6 months before following up with them as requests from other creatives are piling high. Be prepared for rejection, and don't be discouraged. Keep refining your materials, networking, and seeking opportunities to showcase your talent.

Remember, finding the right talent agent is a personal decision, and it's important to do thorough research, ask questions, and ensure that the agency aligns with your career goals and values. It is not just about finding an agent that will take you on, but also an agent that you trust and want to work with.

Be professional, persistent, and proactive in your search for representation, and always prioritize your safety and well-being in any interactions with talent agents or other industry professionals.

Networking as an Artist

As an artist, networking can be a powerful tool for building your career, finding new opportunities, and connecting with other creatives.

Any art event can be a good occasion for networking, as long as you are open to meeting new people and sharing your work. Be sure to bring business cards, a portfolio or samples of your work, and a positive attitude to every event you attend.

Art shows, gallery openings, and other events in your local community are great to connect with artists and art enthusiasts, curators, and gallery owners, and to share your work and learn about new opportunities.

Art fairs and festivals bring together a variety of artists, art dealers, and collectors in one place; art talks and lectures provide breaks to learn about new trends and ideas in the art world; and art charity events support a good cause while also offering a chance for networking with other artists and professionals in the art industry.

Always keep on learning and use art workshops and classes not just to learn new skills and techniques, but also to connect with other artists who share your interests.

Joining artist associations or organizations can help you connect with other artists, stay up-to-date on industry news and trends, and access resources and opportunities. Look for associations or organizations that cater to your specific artistic discipline or style.

Social media platforms such as Instagram, Twitter, and Facebook can be powerful tools for networking as an artist. Share your work, connect with other artists and industry professionals, and engage in online conversations related to your art.

Collaborating with other artists can help you expand your creative network and build new relationships. Look for prospects to collaborate on projects, shows, or events with other artists whose work complements your own.

Networking as a Parent

> It takes a village to raise a child, at least if you don't want to become lonely and crazy.

Networking can be important for parents for several reasons. Networking can create a social support system and help you share experiences, find advice, and build relationships with others who are going through similar challenges.

If you are a new parent, networking can provide opportunities to learn from others. Whether it's attending parenting workshops or participating in online parenting forums, networking can help parents gain knowledge and insight into different parenting styles and techniques. Join parenting groups in your local community, such as mom or dad groups, playgroups, or parenting classes. These groups are great to meet other parents and build relationships with others who have similar interests and experiences.

Attend school events, such as parent-teacher conferences, school plays, or sports games to connect with other parents in your child's school community.

Becoming a parent often also changes your outlook on life and where your priorities are. Networking can help you if you are looking for career prospects or career changes.

Networking can also help parents get involved in their communities. By connecting with other parents and community leaders, you can find volunteer opportunities at your child's school or in your community and become more engaged in local events and activities.

Join online forums or social media groups focused on parenting or family life, such as Peanut or HelloMamas. These forums are there to connect with parents from around the world and gain insight and advice from other parents, as well as give tips about things to do in your area.

Overall, networking can be a valuable tool for parents, providing social support, learning occasions, career development, and community involvement. By building connections with others, parents can gain insight, support, and new opportunities that can help them navigate the challenges of parenthood.

Other books by the author:

www.ingramcontent.com/pod-product-compliance
Lightning Source LLC
Chambersburg PA
CBHW040247220526
45473CB00001B/406